Th. S. Williams

MEMORIAL

OF

HON. THOMAS SCOTT WILLIAMS,

LATE CHIEF-JUSTICE OF CONNECTICUT, AND PRESIDENT OF THE AMERICAN TRACT SOCIETY:

COMPRISING

REV. DR. HAWES' SERMON,

PREACHED IN THE FIRST CHURCH IN HARTFORD,

SABBATH MORNING, DECEMBER 22, 1861;

PROCEEDINGS

OF

THE HARTFORD COUNTY BAR;

JUDGE WILLIAMS' ADDRESS

ON TAKING THE CHAIR AT THE SOCIETY'S ANNIVERSARY, 1852;

AND

SUNDRY BRIEF TESTIMONIALS.

PUBLISHED BY THE

AMERICAN TRACT SOCIETY,

150 NASSAU-STREET, NEW YORK.

SERMON,

BY REV. JOEL HAWES, D. D.

The righteous shall flourish like the palm-tree; he shall grow like a cedar in Lebanon. Those that be planted in the house of the Lord shall flourish in the courts of our God. They shall still bring forth fruit in old age; they shall be fat and flourishing; to show that the Lord is upright: he is my rock, and there is no unrighteousness in him. PSA. 92:12–15.

MANY of my hearers, I presume, on the reading of these words, felt at once that they are strikingly applicable to the loved and venerated man who has just been taken from us, and that his character and life furnish a happy illustration of their spirit and meaning. It is this their suggestive fitness which has led me to the choice of them as the theme of present discourse.

Under the beautiful and instructive imagery of the text, I propose to illustrate the origin, growth, and fruitfulness of a true religious life, as exemplified in the experience and character of a righteous man.

The term "righteous" as used in the text, denotes not merely a man of a correct moral character, but a man of true inward piety, one who is animated with the love of God, and whose character is formed after the spirit and precepts of his word. Such a character is not of self growth; it does not come of nature, fallen and ruined as it is in sin; it is the product of divine grace, the planting of the Lord, and is nurtured, matured, and made fruitful under the culture of his word and providence and Spirit. Hence believers are styled by Isaiah, Trees of righteousness, the planting of the Lord, that he may be glorified. No character grows and thrives so as to bring forth fruit unto God, as represented in the text, which is not of his planting and of his cultivation. Without this, however fair and promising it may be for a time, it will ere long begin to wither and dry up, and like the seed sown in stony places, bring forth no fruit unto perfection.

To indicate the durable felicity and fruitfulness of the persons spoken of in the text, they are likened, you perceive, to the lasting strength and beauty of palm-trees and cedars. These emblems, striking and expressive as they are in our view, must have been much more so in the view of those residing in Palestine and the East, where palms and cedars abounded, and where all their useful properties, whether for beauty, for fruit, for shade, or building material, were familiar to the people. To show the propriety and expressiveness of these emblems, I would just remark, in passing, that the palm is one of the most beautiful and productive trees of the vegetable kingdom. It rises to a great height; retains, even in heat and drought, its fresh foliage; and its crown of broad expanded leaves glittering in the sun, and covering its rich clusters, presents a delightful appearance to the eye of the traveller. It is of slow growth, but lives to a great age, and continues for scores of years to increase in productiveness. The fruit of the palm, in the various forms in which it is used, constitutes a large part of the food of the people where it grows; and it is said by Mr. Gibbon, that the natives have celebrated no less than three hundred and sixty different uses to which the trunk, the branches, the sap, the leaves, and the fruit have been applied.

The cedar also, like the palm, is an

evergreen, and much celebrated in the Scriptures. It is a tree of majestic height and size; spreading out its lofty and graceful branches, and affording a refreshing shade; it thrives even in the most unfavorable situations, and continues to grow for ages; and from the great strength and tenacity of its wide-spread roots, striking deep into the earth, it can withstand the most furious winds and storms that sweep over the mountains of Lebanon, where anciently it grew in extended forests, though very few are found there now.

The palm-tree and cedar, then, are beautiful and expressive emblems to represent the growth, stability, and fruitfulness of those who are properly called the righteous. Those to whom this character belongs, are not of ephemeral, transient growth, appearing well for a time, and then falling away or becoming dry and fruitless. Planted of the Lord, and therefore trees of righteousness, they are rooted and grounded in the deep, rich soil of his grace and truth, and so they continue to grow and bring forth fruit year after year, even to old age. Like the palm-tree and cedar, they may be slow in reaching the period of their full growth and strength: but after that, there is no blight or decay by change of circumstances; they retain their freshness, and flourish on amid heat and drought, abounding more and more in fruits of righteousness to the glory of God and the good of mankind, till he who planted them in his vineyard here below, comes to transfer them to flourish for ever in the paradise above.

Let us pass to the next clause of our text: "Those that be planted in the house of the Lord shall flourish in the courts of our God." This language, we see at once, is highly figurative. I shall not stop to examine the different interpretations that have been put upon it, nor attempt to fix its precise meaning. It relates no doubt to the same class of persons as are mentioned in the preceding verse, the righteous, the true friends of God; and when they are spoken of as planted in the house of the Lord, and flourishing in the courts of our God, the language, I think, is not to be understood as referring to any particular time or place, but as denoting the whole combined system of means and influences, wherever and however employed, by which God renews and sanctifies the hearts of men, places them in his spiritual vineyard, and trains them up for his service and glory. The planting and flourishing point to the beginning and progress of religion in the soul; and the meaning is very similar to that expressed in the words, "first the blade, then the ear, after that the full corn in the ear." The means and influences used to secure this planting and flourishing of the trees of righteousness are many and various; and they operate to produce their effect in very different circumstances and places. The planting intended may take place in the warm, rich soil of a well-conducted Christian family, and many are the plants that spring up and grow there, to flourish afterwards in the courts of God. Or the planting may take place in a Sabbath-school—that too is an admirable vineyard, and well adapted to secure the same result. Or it may take place in the house of God, the sanctuary of the Lord, where his word is preached, his ordinances administered, and the Holy Spirit is given to render the means of grace there enjoyed effectual in bringing souls to God, and fitting them to serve and glorify him in his kingdom. But wherever the planting takes place, whether in the family, the Sabbath-school, or church, there in the spirit, if not in the intent of our text, is the house of the Lord, and there is implanted the principle, the germ of a new life in the soul. And being of God's planting, the work of his Spirit in the inner man, it has in it the vital element, and is sure to grow and bring forth fruits of holiness in the life. Those who are thus planted of God have within them a new divine life; and durability, permanence, are its essential characteristics; and it goes on to thrive and grow in all the graces of the Spirit, till it blooms and flourishes in all the beauties of holiness, in the courts of the Lord, or in those higher and purer attainments of piety which banish doubt, brighten hope, and perfect love in the soul, just, as it were, on the confines of heaven. The flourishing intended in our text is a progressive process. Like the palm-tree, it may be long in reaching its full period of blossom and fruit. But it grows and advances from year to year, till it may truly be said to flourish in the courts of God here below, ready to be transferred to flourish for ever in his courts above.

We must notice another striking expression in our text, "They shall still bring forth fruit in old age; they shall be fat and flourishing." Planted by the living waters of grace, and nourished by the sunshine and rain of heaven, the righteous grow and flourish in hope of glory; their verdure and their fruit are constant, whether in the summer of prosperity or in the winter of adversity; "yea, their very leaf exhales a delightful perfume, by a holy example and conversation; their affections and desires are warm and active, ascending towards the purest and noblest objects—the things of God and heaven." Happy the man whose religion is always progressive, and whose virtues increase with years; who loses not, in the multiplicity of worldly cares and pursuits, the holy fervors of his love, or his living interest in divine things, but goes on burning and shining more and more to the end of his days. A more beautiful sight than this is never seen in our world—a man bringing forth fruit in old age; vigorous and flourishing under the weight of years; buoyant, cheerful, happy, when his sun is just ready to go down; still alive and active in his sphere, interested in the welfare of all around him, and using his last remains of strength to promote their good and the cause of his Saviour. A more beautiful sight than this, I repeat, is not seen upon earth. What a triumph is this of grace; what a testimony to the reality and worth of religion; what an encouragement to others traversing the same way, and what honor does it reflect on the Saviour's name. Ah, these spiritual trees, these trees of God's planting, they flourish in his house or under the means of his appointment, as the natural trees when they are planted in a rich soil, or by rivers of water. They retain their sap and their freshness, and continue to blossom and bring forth fruit even in old age. They may not be as active as they once were, nor fill the offices they once did, nor mingle so freely in public affairs; still, they continue to bring forth fruit, more fruit and better, it may be, than at an earlier period of life—fruit in an increase of tenderness in the sensibilities—fruit in the exercise of more constant and lively spiritual affections—fruit in a visible ripening of all the Christian graces and virtues; in growing humility, and faith, and love; in a warmer interest in the kingdom and glory of Christ; in a growing liberality and readiness to contribute to the benevolent objects of the day; in an increasing love for all the duties of religion, for the Sabbath, for worship, and the ordinances of God's house: fruit, in a word, in a silent yet speaking Christian example; standing forth in the view of the world, as a consistent, devoted, loving follower of the Saviour, clad in the robe of his righteousness, and ripe for heaven. Such is the fruit which those bring forth in old age who have been planted in the house of the Lord, and trained up to flourish in the courts of our God. Their rich clusters hang upon them fresh and abundant as ever, and even when they pass away from us, their fruit still remains to refresh and bless those who survive, even for generations to come.

And now, what is the end, the summing up, the result of all this? The text answers, "To show that the Lord is upright; he is my rock, and there is no unrighteousness in him." The planting of the righteous and their flourishing and bringing forth fruit are not for their sake alone, or principally: they share indeed in the good results, and are made objects of God's everlasting friendship and love; but the ultimate end in view rises infinitely higher than this: it is to show forth the faithfulness of God, his truth, his grace, his unchangeable uprightness in all his dealings with his friends; and this they are constrained gratefully to acknowledge, as from the close of their course they look back upon the way in which the Lord their God has led them, and in the fulness of their hearts they are ready to exclaim, He is my rock, and there is no unrighteousness in him.

I have thus briefly set before you the lessons taught us in the deeply interesting portion of Scripture under consideration. And now, before I proceed to the principal design of this discourse, I can not forbear to suggest a few of the reflections which the subject seems adapted to impress on the mind. And,

1. Observe the beautiful consistency which runs through a true religious life. Such a life has its beginning in the grace of God; it is of his planting; and having this as its origin, it continues to grow and thrive like the palm-tree and cedar, gathering strength and comeliness from year to year, till it is fitted to flourish in the courts of the Lord, or in those higher attainments in truth and holiness which adorn the mature and fully developed Christian character; and then, retaining

its vital freshness and vigor, it continues to bring forth fruit unto God even down to old age, when it is translated from this world to flourish for ever in heaven. This is a true Christian life. A beautiful consistency marks every stage of its development and growth. There is nothing transient, nothing impulsive, nothing merely emotional or ephemeral about it. It is based on principle; rooted and grounded in the truth; nurtured and strengthened by it; and watered by the dews of the Spirit, it expands and grows into fruitfulness in all the Christian graces to the glory of God and the honor of religion. This is the type of Christian character and life contemplated in the gospel—the type which all should aspire to attain, and which many have attained, some in the midst of ourselves, to the joy and comfort of their own hearts and the honor of the Christian name. And of whom can this be said more truly than of our deceased friend? Consistency was indeed a bright gem in his character, and it shone with increasing lustre till the last.

2. No earthly blessing is so great as to be descended from a pious ancestry, to be nurtured and trained in the house of the Lord, or amid the means and influences of a true Christian parentage. I am no believer in the transmission of Christian character, or that piety is inherited by children from their parents; but I have strong faith in the covenant promises of God made to them that love and fear his name. These promises relate not to parents alone, but to their children and their posterity in coming years, down to many generations. I have not time to develop this thought, or to follow it out in illustration and proof. I must content myself here with

simply referring you to the unquestionable fact that religion, true piety, does, to a remarkable and most encouraging extent, run in the line of a Christian ancestry, of a pious, godly parentage. This I have observed, with growing interest, during the whole course of my ministry; and from year to year I have seen more and more truth, as well as poetic beauty, in the lines of Cowper, penned by him on the receipt of his mother's picture.

> "My boast is, not that I deduce my birth
> From loins enthroned and rulers of the earth;
> But higher far my proud pretensions rise,
> The son of parents passed into the skies."

Ah, this being planted in the house of the Lord finds its true spiritual meaning in being born of Christian parents; in being surrounded in childhood and youth by the means of grace and salvation enjoyed in a well-regulated Christian household, over which praying parents preside, going before their offspring in the way to heaven, and winning them to follow by wise instruction, true prayer, and holy example. Where this is the case, children are very likely to grow up in the nurture and training thus afforded them, till they flourish in the courts of God, and finally ascend to meet their parents and other ancestors who have gone before them to heaven.

3. Another reflection suggested by our subject is the inestimable value of an early established, right character. Such a character is not inherited; it does not come by chance, nor grow up without toil and effort. It is the combined result of right feelings, right purposes, and right habits, carried out in a life of integrity, honor, and usefulness; of devotion to the service of God and the good of mankind. Such a character planted in the house of the Lord is sure to flourish in the courts

of our God. It will grow like the palm-tree and cedar; its ripest and most precious fruits are found in advancing age. Then it is seen bearing rich clusters—freshness of health, cheerfulness, contentment, happiness; intelligence, piety, all bright in the clear sunshine of faith and hope, ready to be translated and consummated in heaven. A character like this is of more value than all the treasures of earth. Mere talents, learning, genius, social position, and wealth are worth nothing in comparison with it. As a means of success in life, of securing the confidence and respect of mankind, and opening sources of usefulness and happiness in this world, a character like that just indicated, or even one approximating to it, throws into distance and shade all other means of earthly enjoyment and influence. To a young man, a young lawyer for example, just setting out in the world, a character for integrity, for fidelity, honor, and honesty, is the best possible passport he can have for success in his calling. It will set him forward in business, draw around him clients, give him an influence with the jury and the court and the community at large, which nothing else can secure to him. As proof of this I might refer you to the example of the venerated and honored man who has just departed from us. Character was the great secret of his success and influence in life. He was known to be a man of high integrity; an honest, reliable, faithful man: he showed this character in the commencement of his professional career; he maintained it untarnished, nay, with growing lustre through the whole of his course. Hence the confidence, the respect, the esteem, and great influence which all who knew him, indeed the whole community, were ever ready to accord to him. I shall have occasion to refer to this again.

It may seem a digression from the train of remark I have been pursuing, but I can not forbear to observe,

4. That real Christians may be expected, as they advance in age and draw near the time of their departure, to discover in themselves and show to others a growing spirituality and meetness for heaven. So it was in a marked degree with our deceased friend. As he advanced in life he continued to grow in grace, and bring forth fruit unto God, preparing for his exit and ripening for heaven. And when the summons came he was ready. And so, I believe, it always is with true Christians, such as in any measure answer to the description given in our text. I can not better illustrate this than in the language of the great Dr. Owen. "There are two

things," he says, "which those who, after a long profession of the gospel, are entering into the confines of eternity, do long for and desire. The one is, that all their breaches may be repaired, their decays recovered, and their backslidings healed. The other is, that they may have fresh springs of spiritual life, and vigorous actings of divine grace in spiritual mindedness, holiness, and faithfulness, unto the praise of God, the honor of the gospel, and the increase of their own peace and joy. These things they value more than all the world and all that is in it; about these things are their thoughts and contrivances exercised night and day. Those with whom it is otherwise, whatever they may pretend, are in the dark unto themselves and their condition; for it is in the nature of this grace to grow and increase unto the end. As rivers, the nearer they come unto the ocean, whither they tend, the more they increase their waters and speed their course, so will grace grow more freely and fully in its near approach to the ocean of glory. That is not saving," he says, "which doth not so." He adds in another place, "If a man hath made a great appearance of religion in his former or younger days, and when he is growing into age becomes dead, cold, worldly, selfish—if he have no fresh springs of spiritual life in him, it is an evidence that he hath in him a barren heart, and that he was never really fruitful unto God." These are weighty thoughts; I commend them to the serious consideration of all who hear me. How far our deceased friend was removed from blight and barrenness need not be stated to those who have observed his course since he made a profession of religion, and connected with this church twenty-seven years ago. That course was steadily progressive, more and more marked with spirituality and faithfulness unto God till it was finished, and he was called home to the presence of his Saviour in heaven.

5. Another remark is suggested by our subject: How interesting and beautiful a sight is an "old disciple of Christ," one who during a long life has been faithful in duty, still fresh in his age, flourishing like the palm-tree, bearing fruit unto God, ripe to be removed to the paradise above. And this naturally brings me back to the words placed at the head of this discourse; and as I remarked at the beginning, all who hear me, I presume, feel that they are strikingly applicable to the departed friend to whom both duty and affection demand that we should render our public tribute of honor and respect. I shall not pronounce his eulogy.

He needs not that from me; and any thing of the kind would be an offence to the whole spirit and character of the man. But I may speak of the grace of God that made him what he was, and of the providence of God that employed him as an instrument of accomplishing so much good in his day and generation.

I know of no man of whom it may be more truly said than of Thomas Scott Williams, that he was planted in the house of the Lord, and he surely did flourish in the courts of our God. He was born at Wethersfield, June 26th, 1777, of highly respectable and devotedly Christian parents, and his ancestors in long succession were distinguished as among the friends and followers of Christ. He was the youngest but one of eleven children, all of whom are now gone; and all were hopefully Christians and members of the church. And this shows the truth of what I have before said, that no earthly blessing is so great as to be descended from pious ancestors, born of parents devoted to the service and kingdom of God. I have often said of him of whom I here speak, that he was from the first a favored child of Providence. Nursed in the bosom of piety, and trained in his earliest days in the midst of kindly Christian influences, he grew up with those elements of character germinating and flourishing within, which made him what he was in subsequent life. An incident may be mentioned here, interesting as an element in his early training.

A Scotch lady of high intelligence and of warm, devoted piety, resided in the family of Sheriff Williams, the father of Thomas. It was so that he was committed almost to the entire care of this lady for the first nine years of his life. Judge

Williams often spoke of the instruction, example, and prayers of this estimable Christian woman as having been a great blessing to him in moulding his character and directing his course in life. The child, in his case, was eminently the father of the man. He was graduated at Yale college in 1794, when he was but little past seventeen years old, too young, as he often remarked, to have reaped the full advantage of a college course. But always correct as he was in his morals and diligent in his studies, he laid the foundation of those habits of application and persevering effort which subsequently raised him to such eminence in his profession. After pursuing the study of law, first at Litchfield under Judge Reeve, and then at Windham under Chief-Justice Swift, he was admitted to the bar in 1798, and commenced practice in Mansfield. In 1803 he removed to this city,

ing, of his reputation before the public, and of the impression he left on my mind after an acquaintance with him of more than forty years.

His mind was of a high order, clear, discriminating, and powerful in argumentation, distinguished more for strong common-sense, than for fine-spun abstraction, or nice metaphysical acumen. He had a sound practical judgment, and a ready retentive memory, in which were treasured the results of his study and observation. He was an indefatigable student, and a great worker in his profession. Thoroughly versed in the principles of law, he was able to develop and apply them with great success. He carefully studied and prepared his cases, and when he appeared in court he knew just what to do with them—what strong points he had to make, and what lesser ones might be passed over. In speaking at the bar, he showed great earnestness and sincerity, as if he really believed what he said, and meant to make others believe it. His conceded knowledge of the law, his clear intelligence, and his downright integrity and honesty of purpose gave him great influence both with the jury and the bench; and the remark has been made by one of his profession, that so great was the confidence reposed in his judgment, that his opinion would be taken for law, even if there were no law. As a judge, he was eminently upright, impartial, and just; and hence his judicial decisions, wherever known—and they are widely known—are held of great authority. Every thing that savored of finesse, of artful management to carry a purpose, whether at the bar or on the bench, he held in utter abhorrence, and no one trait of his character was more manifest and all-pervading than open, frank, decided integrity, and a genial kindness of nature, which won for him the confidence of his clients, and the respect and esteem of all who knew him. His manners, dignified and self-respectful, presented a beautiful combination of ease, simplicity, and benevolence; and these, beaming forth from the eye and from the whole aspect of the man, made him, together with his rich and instructive conversation, one of the most agreeable of companions, and could hardly fail to secure for him the love as well as the respect of all who were much in his society. His transparent purity of character and simplicity of manners, his entire freedom from all ostentation and show—and these he carried with him into all the relations and intercourse of life—made him in this respect a model man, a most useful and instructive example to all around him.

I pass over the numerous and various civil offices which he was called to fill during the long life he spent with us, as too well known to need being noticed here, remarking only that the duties connected with them he always discharged with great fidelity and promptness, so as to secure the approbation and confidence of the entire community. As a citizen, a civilian, a statesman, a patriot, he was firm and decided in his views and sentiments, adhering inflexibly to what he believed to be true and right; but he was no partisan, no wily politician, or bigoted opposer of all who differed from him in opinion. At every subject bearing on the welfare, whether of the city, the state, or the country at large, he looked with a careful, discriminating eye; and in forming his judgment, he took counsel, "not of prejudice, not of party, not of personal self-interest, nor yet of the wishes of friends, nor of the opposition of enemies, but of an honest devotion to the public good, under the guidance of conscience and of God." I never knew a man more entirely decided in adhering to what he believed to be right and duty than Judge Williams; yet there was so much integrity and kindness mingled with his decision and firmness, that he made very few if any enemies, and those who differed from him were constrained to concede to him the credit of great conscientiousness, and of a sincere desire to do what he believed to be pleasing to God and promotive of the best interests of his fellow-men.

But I dwell on this part of my subject too long. I pass to that which comes more appropriately within my sphere, the moral and religious character of our departed friend.

Trained up by Christian parents, and

surrounded in all his early years by Christian influences, he came forward into life with a fair moral character, with much respect for religion, and a general belief in its doctrines. But like many other young men similarly situated, religion was not allowed to have any saving place in his heart, or any decided influence over his life, as a supreme governing principle. Pressed as he was incessantly, after he came to this city, by a large and continually increasing business, he gave himself but little time, it is believed, to think on his relations to God and the concerns of salvation. He admitted the great truths of the gospel in his understanding; but to their renewing power, to the necessity of a living, indwelling piety as a condition of pardon and acceptance with God, he was, in his own view, a stranger. So it was when I first knew him, and so it was essentially till 1834. In the winter and spring of that year, it pleased God to shed down upon the congregation the gracious influences of his Spirit, and a general attention was awakened to the concerns of the soul. Among the number—and they were largely persons of mature age—who were moved to take up the subject of religion as a direct personal concern, were Judge Williams and his first wife, a woman of very estimable character, but not then, as she believed, a Christian. The result was, that after long earnest and anxious inquiry, they both came to a calm and settled hope in Christ, accepted him by faith as their Saviour, and in the course of the summer, they, with about sixty others, united with the church by a public profession of religion. From that time his path was like that of the shining light that shineth more and more unto the perfect day. His religion was more of principle than of emotion, more of a steady, set purpose to do what is right and pleasing to God, and useful to his fellow-men, than of mere impulse and feeling. He had indeed a heart of great tenderness and sympathy, and often his affections would be moved even to tears, when the touching themes of the gospel were brought home to his bosom, or he was appealed to by some object of sorrow and suffering.

In 1836 he was elected a deacon in the church. His natural modesty and self-distrust made him hesitate long before he accepted the appointment. But with what propriety, dignity, and conscientious fidelity he performed the duties of his office, to the honor of religion and the prosperity of this church, need not be stated here. Besides officiating at the table of the Lord with his brethren, his ministries of kindness, of counsel and charity in private, were many and frequent; and long will he be remembered by the poor and needy as a kind and generous benefactor. And it is an affecting fact, that the last service he ever performed in the church was, to assist in bearing the symbols of the Saviour's love to his fellow-worshippers.

Shortly after he united with the church he entered the Sabbath-school as a teacher, and there for more than a quarter of a century, he was from Sabbath to Sabbath at the head of his Bible-class, thoroughly prepared by previous study to impart to its members the rich treasures of God's word, and of his own well-stored mind. Never absent except by necessity, and always in his place in time, he instructed large numbers of young men in the elements of God's truth and salvation, who will cherish his memory with grateful affection as long as they live, and many of them for ever. The good he accomplished in this humble office, as many esteem it, by his example and instructions, can never be known till it is revealed at the last day.

And here, I can not forbear to speak of Judge Williams' respect for the Sabbath. He was early taught by his parents to reverence the Lord's day. This grew up with him as a habit, and during all his professional life, before he became a member of the church, it was his custom, as I am told, to lay aside all professional and secular books, with newspapers and the like, as not suited to Sabbath-day reading, and to take up some religious work, such for example as the Christian Observer, to occupy his time in the interim of public worship. After he professed religion, the Sabbath assumed a still more sacred character in his view, and was kept in a more conscientious,

Christian manner. He loved the Sabbath; he esteemed it the holy of the Lord, honorable, and a delight. "To his eye, it bore the King's image and superscription. It was a day set apart for holy uses; and accepting, in its just import, the saying of our Saviour, 'The Sabbath was made for man,' he studiously consecrated it to the purposes prescribed by its beneficent Donor, to the concerns of the soul, and the sublime realities of the life which awaits us beyond the grave." He loved the house of God and its worship, and was always in his place, morning and afternoon, in serious and devout attendance on divine service.

And to these well-spent Sabbaths we must look for many of the influences which contributed to mould, as well his intellectual and social, as his elevated moral and religious character. Let not his example in this respect be forgotten.

In a conversation I had with him not long before his death, he expressed his deep concern at the growing neglect of the Sabbath and of public worship, even by too many who profess to be Christians. He viewed it as a fact portentous of evil, and so it is; and I would here hold up the example of our venerated friend and servant of Christ, now gone from the midst of us to the rest and worship of heaven, to stay a practice fraught only with evil, and to engage all who hear me to do as he did during a long life, to remember the Sabbath-day to keep it holy.

Judge Williams was an admirable model of industry. He lived by rule. Every hour had its duty, and every duty its hour, and it was in no small part this habit of punctuality and order, entering as it did into all his plans and pursuits of life, which enabled him to accomplish so great an amount of work in his day, both as a lawyer and as a Christian man. Though long retired from public life, he was scarcely less busy or less occupied than he was before. His circle of active duty was changed, but not forsaken. Age came upon him more by adding to his years than by any change it wrought in his bodily or mental powers. He retained the freshness, cheerfulness, and vigor of earlier years in a remarkable manner. He kept his own heart warm and active by keeping it in contact with the living, moving world around him. He did not retire into himself as age came on, nor become misanthropic and selfish and complaining because things did not go just as he wished, or just as they did when he was younger and bore a part in them. He looked out upon the church and the world with a hopeful eye, and continued to the last to take a lively interest in all that related to the kingdom of Christ and the good of his fellow-men. And this I doubt not was a principal cause of the green and happy old age which he so eminently enjoyed. As years came on, each added to the treasures of his well-spent life. And I here may be permitted to repeat what I said of him in a sermon I preached at Saratoga, a little more than a year since, as it expresses what I am sure you will all admit to be true. I was speaking of him as an example of the happy effects of a well-spent life. He is now, I said, in his eighty-fourth year, cheerful, healthy, active; found at the head of his Bible-class every Sabbath-morning; always in his place in the sanctuary, and at our occasional religious meetings, ready to bear a part in them; his heart warm and sympathizing as ever in all good objects, and his hand ready to help them forward; his influence, though less public than formerly, is hardly less effective and beneficent in the noiseless teachings of a consistent ripened Christian character: he stands forth a fine example of the rich treasures which a well-spent life gathers around itself in its close, ready to be transferred to enrich and adorn the life which is to come.

I may not omit to remark here, that such were the social affections of our deceased friend, and such his domestic habits, that his home could not fail to be a happy one. And so it was. Marked with an easy, generous hospitality, a large circle of relatives and friends were attracted to it, to enjoy the society and kindly attentions of the family, and among them none were more welcome or treated with greater kindness than the minister and the missionary.

That Judge Williams had a large, generous, outflowing heart will readily be inferred from what has already been said. This was indeed a shining trait in his character, and it brought him into close communion with the various benevolent associations of our age and country. Blessed with an abundance of this world's goods, he felt himself to be a steward of God, bound to use all that was entrusted to him in obedience to his will, and for the glory of his name. And he was, in an eminent degree, a faithful steward. It is known that, for many years, he has acted on the principle, not of accumulating, but expending, the whole of his income, and often he went beyond it in charitable benefactions. He was one of the most generous and cheerful of givers. I have often said of him, that I never knew a man whom it cost so little to do good. Doing good seemed to be a kind of instinct, a natural impulse, not a self-denial, but a happiness to him. He never frowned, nor fretted, nor uttered untrue excuses, as is too common, when a charity or a contribution was asked of him. He received every applicant with kindness, heard his statement with patience, and if he approved he gave, otherwise he dismissed him in good nature. To all the benevolent operations of the day he was a large and a constant contributor. Besides his private charities, which were many, and constantly dropping as the rain and the dew to relieve the needy and the suffering, he was always ready to bear a generous part in founding and sustaining the humane, the benevolent, and educational institutions of the city, and all other enterprises adapted and designed to promote its material prosperity.

He felt a deep interest in the Redeemer's kingdom, and he gave largely of his substance to aid in spreading the gospel through the world. The cause of home and foreign missions ever lay near his heart, as indeed did all the kindred institutions of the day, having in view the common object of extending the knowledge of Christ over the earth; and his yearly contributions to these societies will be greatly missed, unless others come forward with a largely increased generosity, to make up the deficiency. Who among us will do this?

And now, if he were present of whom I have been speaking, or could he make his voice heard from the spirit-world whither he is gone, there is no sentiment I have uttered which he would so readily approve and apply to himself, as that with which our text closes: *To show that the Lord is upright: he is my rock, and there is no unrighteousness in him.* My good deeds, my virtues and privileges and blessings, what are they all but the fruit of the goodness and mercy of God bestowed on me, a poor unworthy sinner? All I was and did on earth that was right, and all I am and enjoy now in the presence of my Saviour, I ascribe to his rich grace; I claim no part of it as a matter of merit; all was and is of grace, and to God my rock be all the praise.

This leads me to a closing remark, that among the virtues which adorned the character of our deceased friend, humility held a prominent place. He seldom spoke of himself, and never in terms of self-praise or commendation. He had a deep and an abiding sense of his personal unworthiness and guilt in the sight of God, and rested all his hope of salvation—not confident, but sustaining and comforting—on the mercy and grace of Christ his Redeemer. He held in firm faith the great distinguishing doctrines of the gospel, but without the least mixture of bigotry or exclusiveness. He was much stricter and more unsparing in judging of himself than of others, and a most amiable trait it was in his character, that he was much more inclined to extenuate and apologize for the failings of others than to exaggerate and condemn them with too great severity. He rarely spoke disparagingly of any one, and never with a fault-finding, ill temper. His religion, as I have before said, was with him an indwelling principle. It pervaded his heart, his character, his life. It led him daily to his closet, there to pray unto his Father in secret; and to the family altar, there to offer the morning and evening sacrifice; and to the church on the Sabbath, there to worship God with his people. In a word, it went with him into all the relations and walks of life, and had much, very much, to do in forming him to that symmetry, that harmony of all the susceptibilities and powers of his nature, which made him so complete, or I would say, in the language of the Bible, so perfect a man. It revealed itself, not so much by any specific, movable, or transient form, as by its influence upon the whole man; "like a light behind a beautiful transparency, which, unseen itself, illuminates every line of the artist's handiwork." "It might be seen in his temper, his conduct, his manners, in all that he did, and in all that he said. No trumpet, nor phylactery was needed to announce its presence; his serene and venerable aspect, his suavity, his cheerfulness, his overflowing kindness, his prompt and generous interest in others' wants and sorrows, and the whole tone of his conversation, whether on public affairs or matters of personal concern, all betrayed the intercourse of his soul with heaven, and awakened the feeling, Thou also wast with Jesus of Nazareth."

This great and good man has gone to his reward. The summons came unexpectedly to his friends, though not to himself,* and it found him all ready to

* One of the first papers found in Judge Williams' private desk in his office after his death, was the following memorandum, which had been so placed in a manuscript-book that it could not fail to be noticed at once by Mrs. Williams. It evidently had been recently written, doubtless on Monday or Tuesday, the 2d or 3d of December, 1861, on each of which days—having been confined to his house by an apparently slight cold for several days the previous week—he spent an hour in his office, never entering it again after Tuesday, December 3d.

"I know that your memory will bring to your mind many passages of Scripture full of consolation for the loss you have sustained. But from uninspired writings, none has occurred to me more appropriate than the following:

"'Thou art gone to the grave, but we will not deplore thee,
Since God was thy refuge, thy ransom, thy guide;
He gave thee, he took thee, and he will restore thee,
And death hath no sting, since the Saviour hath died.'"

go, his loins girded about, and his lamp trimmed and burning. His sickness was brief, and not painful. The powers of life were exhausted, the vital spark flickered for a time where it had burnt so long and so brightly; then like an expiring taper, it went out, and he passed away. His sun went down full-orbed and bright, without a spot or a shade

The opening paragraphs of Judge Williams' last will also exhibit his calm anticipation of death, and seem peculiarly touching to those who appreciate the circumstances under which they were written. Hon. Francis Parsons, a nephew whom Judge Williams had long loved and relied on as a son, died after a brief illness, ten days before the date of the will.

"I, Thomas S. Williams, of Hartford, at present, by the blessing of God, being in good health and of sound and disposing mind, but reminded by the death of all my brothers and sisters, and now by a more unexpected stroke, as well as by my age and infirmities, that my time is short—do make this my last will and testament.

"I commit my soul to God who gave it, and my body to the earth, hoping for a glorious resurrection with the just, through the merits of our Lord and Saviour Jesus Christ."

upon it, and has risen, we doubt not, to shine for ever amid the splendors of an eternal day. Oh, rise some other light, to fill the place of that which has just left its orbit here below, to shine in a higher and nobler sphere above.

I have thus endeavored to pay an humble tribute to the memory of one whom we all respected, whom we all loved. The death of Judge Williams has brought upon us a great bereavement and sorrow. The pastor feels it; this church and congregation feel it; the whole community feels it. Yet has he left us much for which we are called to render thanksgiving and praise to God—his high integrity as a man, his bright example as a Christian, his prayers and the influence of his wide-spread and beneficent deeds, continued through so long a life, closed by so peaceful and happy a death. Let us all profit by the treasure thus bequeathed to us, and follow him as he followed Christ. Sad and frequent of late have been the notes sounded through this congregation, calling us all to prepare for the time of our departure. Parsons, Trumbull, Storrs, Warburton, Fitch, not to mention honored and loved names among the female members of this church—all these and others, within a few months, have been called away; and now Williams is numbered with them. Surely God must have a meaning in these striking dispensations of his providence towards us. And what is that meaning, if it be not that we hear the voice of his warning, speed our work while it is day, and prepare for the night of death when we can no more work? Especially does it become him who utters these words to take the full meaning of them to himself, seeing that to-day he finishes the seventy-second year of his life, and as he looks round on his congregation, scarcely recognizes more than two or three who bore any part in his call and ordination, and very few who were present on that occasion. The flight of years, and the departure of dear and loved ones, once the members of my flock, admonish me that my sun hastens to its going down, and will soon sink beneath the horizon. Let me notice these signals, and be ready to meet the event of which they forewarn me. Cheered may I be, as I go on to finish the brief remainder of my course, with the blessed hope of meeting in heaven the many, many dear friends who have ascended to that world before me.

PROCEEDINGS

OF

THE HARTFORD COUNTY BAR.

AT a meeting of the members of the Hartford county bar, held in the court-room on Wednesday noon, Dec. 18, 1861, for the purpose of expressing their respect for the late Chief-Justice Williams, R. D. Hubbard, Esq., presiding, Wm. Hungerford, Esq., offered the following resolutions:

"WHEREAS, after a life of untiring and successful industry, of eminent purity, of great excellence and religious consistency, the Hon. THOMAS S. WILLIAMS, late Chief-Justice of this state, has, at a mature and ripe old age, been gathered to his rest; therefore,

"*Resolved*, That few men have left behind them higher claims to public respect and esteem, and none a stronger hold upon the grateful remembrance of the legal profession, of which he was so long an honored and distinguished member. His industry, untiring zeal, and professional ability and integrity; his learning, wisdom, and conscientiousness in the administration of the laws; the purity and excellence of his public and private life, afford alike an imperishable example to the living, to guide them in the sure paths to success, honor, happiness, and a useful, well-spent life.

"*Resolved*, That in his death this bar has lost one of its most esteemed members; the community in which he lived, one ever ready to coöperate and bear his share to promote its interests and advance its prosperity; the young, a faithful friend, counsellor, and guide; the charities of the day and the great benevolent institutions of the age, a systematic, cheerful, and liberal supporter; the religious community and the church, an earnest, sincere, and devoted Christian; and the world, an excellent and good man.

"*Resolved*, That in respect for his memory, we will attend his funeral in a body.

"*Resolved*, That the foregoing resolutions be entered upon the records of this bar; and a copy thereof, signed by the chairman and countersigned by the secretary, be transmitted to the family of the deceased, in assurance of our sincere condolence and sympathy on account of the great loss they have sustained."

Mr. Hungerford then spoke as follows:

JUDGE WILLIAMS entered and was graduated at Yale college at a much earlier period of his life than most young men who receive the honors of that institution. He took his degree in 1794. He afterwards commenced, and for some time pursued his studies preparatory for admission to the bar, under the tuition of Judge Reeve of Litchfield, and completed them under that of Judge Swift of Windham. For a few years after his admission to the bar, he resided in the town of Mansfield, in the county of Tolland, and then removed to and permanently located himself in this city, where he ever after resided until the time of his death.

After he came to this city, he pursued his profession with great industry, and rose very rapidly to distinction. At my first acquaintance with him, about forty years since, he had attained to and stood in the first rank His reputation was then well established and known throughout the state. He early acquired a very high standing, not only for learning and talents, but for integrity and candor. As a counsellor, his advice was much and extensively sought for, and confided in when obtained. In giving his legal opinions he was exceedingly careful. If doubts existed in his own mind as to the law, he industriously examined the authorities which he supposed to be applicable to the case in reference to which he was consulted, until the doubt was removed; or, if after such investigation it still remained, he so informed his client. No one who obtained his opinion, whether coinciding with his own views or wishes or not, entertained a doubt but that he was honestly advised. As a prudent and safe counsellor, no one in the state enjoyed or possessed a higher reputation.

In the preparation of his cases for trial he was remarkably thorough and faithful, and much distinguished for his attainments in legal science. As an advocate he was ardent. Feeling a deep interest in the cause of his client, he argued his cause with much zeal—never, however, suffering himself to exceed the rules of propriety or decorum, or to transgress those of the court. To his clients he was always accessible, ready and patient to hear them, and anxious to ascertain as far as possible the real facts in the cause in which he was engaged.

Among his contemporaries and competitors were men of much eminence for their attainments and talents in the legal profession; and it may well be doubted whether, at any period of the history of this state, the bar could command a greater array of learning or ability than while Judge Williams was a member of it, and in practice. To stand side by side with the most prominent men of the profession at that time, was no small honor. By his unflinching integrity, his extensive legal attainments, and great ability, Judge Williams acquired the confidence of the court and jury in an uncommon degree, and was a most successful advocate.

In 1829 he was appointed Judge, and in 1834, Chief-Justice of the Supreme court of this state. The Legislature could not have made a more judicious or popular choice. He brought to the bench a very unusual combination of qualifications peculiarly fitting him for the station. He had accumulated an ample fund of legal science; had become very familiar with authorities, and especially with the decisions, laws, and practice of our own state; and with these he united a most conscientious regard to the faithful discharge of his duty, and an uncommon share of good common-sense. He well understood that "the law as a practical science" could "not take notice of melting lines, nice discriminations, and evanescent quantities." He correctly supposed the laws to be made up of rules designed to regulate the conduct of those who were subject to them, and that they should, as far as possible, be plain, intelligible, and capable of being reduced to practice; and he did much himself to produce this result. By the aid of a strong, clear, and discriminating mind, he was enabled to make, and did make a very just and proper application of authorities. Metaphysical refinements and hair-splitting distinctions had little influence with him. He ever paid strict attention to testimony in the cases brought before him for decision, and unusual skill in weighing it and eliciting the truth when different portions of it came in conflict. He listened with patience to the arguments of counsel, and was not only ready, but anxious to hear whatever could be urged upon either side, so long as any reasonable doubt existed as to the law, or any light could be reflected upon the subject of discussion. The difference between argument and sophistry he readily detected. In court he presided with much dignity and propriety, uniformly courteous to his associates upon the bench, to the jury, the bar, and all in any wise connected with him in the administration of justice, and thereby not only secured to himself the respect and good-will of all, but strict order and regard to the rules of propriety and decorum in the court in which he presided. In his decisions he was exceedingly impartial. He ever looked at the case, and not at the parties. It may, I think, with great truth be asserted, that he had no "respect of persons in judgment." He heard "the small as well as the great." He brought to the bench the same habits of industry which he had at the bar, and in his decisions rarely erred. Those made by him upon the circuit were, in a few instances only, reversed or overruled upon a review in the higher court. He had, in an almost unexampled degree, the confidence of the community in which he lived, and may justly be deemed to have been a model judge. The decisions of the Supreme court, made while he was a member of it, and contained in the Connecticut Reports, commencing in the seventh, terminating in the eighteenth, and extending through the intermediate volumes, will furnish a lasting memorial of his judicial qualifications. In 1847, Judge Williams, having arrived at the age of seventy years, became, under the Constitution of this state, incapable of retaining his seat any longer upon the bench. He then retired from his official labors, but not from his labors of love and good-will to his fellow-men.

A most prominent trait in the character of Judge Williams, and which gave lustre to all his others, was that deep religious sentiment which seemed to pervade his whole soul, and control all his actions. In 1834, the year in which he was appointed Chief-Justice, he made a public profession of religion; but he did not suppose that he had, by making an open avowal of his faith, performed his whole duty. Religion was not with him a mere matter of theory or speculation. He reduced the duties which it enjoined to practice, and exhibited its influence in all the walks and relations of life. He was a most liberal patron of the great benevolent institutions of the day, at the same time abounding in more private charities. In performing these acts of benevolence and charity, he sounded no trumpet before him. They were all done in the spirit of the scriptural injunction, not to let his left hand know what his right hand did. As was said of one in ancient times, he had always rather be good than to seem so. He was utterly devoid of every thing like ostentation or pride. Meekness and humility marked all his conduct. His purse and his heart were alike open to every good object. To most liberal contributions of his property for benevolent purposes, he added his own unremitted personal efforts, and these he continued until his last sickness. No station was too exalted or too humble for him, if it presented a sphere in which he could do good to his fellow-men. And now, after most faithfully performing the duties of the various stations to which he has been called, and in all the relations of life eminently illustrating the excellency of the religion which he professed, greatly revered, beloved, and respected, he has closed his earthly career. He has left the world a character without a stain, and, as I think I may safely assert, not an enemy behind.

William R. Cone, Esq., said substantially:

I approve most heartily of every sentiment contained in the resolutions offered. These links which connect us with the past are being so rapidly severed, one after another, that I find myself here to-day standing almost in the very foremost ranks of the living members of this bar.

Five of the number once connected with this bar—I might indeed count six*—have

* The five referred to are Francis Parsons, Lucius F. Robinson, Wm. L. Storrs, Joseph Trumbull, and Thomas S. Williams.

The sixth referred to is Charles J. Russ; and since this meeting of the Hartford county bar, Henry L. Miller, another of their number, has died.

been taken away within these nine months. So our ranks are being thinned, as one and another of our number fall out by the way; and to-day we are met to pay our tribute of respect, and bear our testimony to the eminence, excellence, and spotless character of the eldest of them all, one who has lived eighty-five years—a long life—and who, during that long and eventful period in the history of the past, and in this age of wonderful progress, has exerted an influence as widespread, and filled a space in the affections and esteem of those who knew him, and the community in which he dwelt, as large as was ever exerted and ever filled by any other man in this state. First as a thorough, industrious, astute, and safe lawyer and counsellor; then as an upright, influential, and reliable statesman; after that as a conscientious judge and the Chief-Justice of the state; always as a prominent citizen, devoted to every interest, and ready to engage in every enterprise calculated to advance and promote the prosperity of the community and city in which he so long had his home; and during these latter years as a devoted Christian, earnest and zealous in every good word and work in his Master's cause.

When I came to this city as a school-boy in 1826, Thomas S. Williams, as he was then familiarly called here, was without a rival at this bar, and I might almost say in the state. And when, in 1832, I returned again to commence my profession here, the ermine had fallen upon his shoulders; and as a judge, none ever brought to the bench a greater store of available learning, and none ever administered the law with greater wisdom, integrity, impartiality, and conscientiousness than did he.

And then, when at the age of seventy he became legally disqualified from longer occupying his place upon the bench, he entered with the same earnestness, devotion, and zeal upon the work of doing good; and I have no man in mind that has done more, no man that has done as much by his influence, his counsels, his labors, and his contributions to forward the great religious charities and other great benevolent enterprises of the age in which he lived, as has Judge Williams. His influence as a good man has been felt everywhere as no other man's has, always in favor of progress, and always on the right side. No undertaking in the way of doing good too stupendous, no labor too arduous or too humble, no station too exalted or place too small or too low, for him to undertake or for him to occupy in his Master's work.

The liberality of his charities when any great and good work needed his aid, was never restricted. He wrote his thousands as some do their tens, twenties, and fifties, when the magnitude of the enterprise required it; and I could point to other evidences, if there was time, that the magnitude of any good work did not deter him from undertaking it.

His earnest devotion to the duties of instructing a Bible-class of young men, where Sabbath after Sabbath for these many last years he has been regularly found at his post, attests his readiness to occupy any place where he could be the instrument of doing good; and multitudes there are of young men in this city and elsewhere, who will rise up and bless his memory because of the good influences they have enjoyed under his teachings.

A good man, yes, my friends, a good man has been gathered home to his rest, like a shock of corn fully ripe for the harvest. His memory will live, and his influence will be felt through all time; for the influence of a good man, such a man, as an example for us and others to imitate, lives always, and will live for ever.

Messrs. Seth Terry, Ex-Judge Ellsworth, Charles Whittlesey, J. H. Holcomb, and R. R. Phelps, each in brief terms spoke of the high and well-deserved reputation of Judge Williams. The resolutions were unanimously adopted.

SUMMARY FACTS

OF JUDGE WILLIAMS' LIFE, FROM THE REPORT OF THE AMERICAN TRACT SOCIETY, MAY, 1862.

Chief-Justice Thomas Scott Williams, LL. D., was born at Wethersfield, Connecticut, June 26, 1777, and was the son of Ezekiel Williams, high-sheriff of the county. At 17 he graduated at Yale college, and after attending the lectures of Judge Reeves at Litchfield, studied law with Chief-Justice Swift of Windham county. Removing to Hartford in 1803, he commenced his long career of usefulness and honor. He was seven times elected to the state legislature, of which he was six years the clerk; from 1817 to 1819 he was a member of Congress, and from 1831 to 1835 was Mayor of Hartford. In 1829 he was appointed Associate Judge of the Supreme Court of Errors, and in 1834 was appointed Chief-Justice, which office he filled with high acceptance till his resignation in 1847; his decisions being quoted by our most eminent jurists. In 1812 he married Delia, daughter of Oliver Ellsworth, Chief-Justice of the United States. She died in 1840, and he afterwards married Martha M. Coit, daughter of the late Elisha Coit of New York. He departed this life on Sabbath morning, December 15, 1861, at the advanced age of eighty-four.

From 1848, for more than thirteen years till his death, he was the esteemed President of the American Tract Society, of which from its formation he had been a firm friend. He gave the Society not only his wise counsels and active coöperation, but his constant and liberal contributions; leaving it a legacy of $5,000 at his death. He also bequeathed $5,000 to the American Board of Foreign Missions, of which he was long the cherished Vice-president; $5,000 to the Home Missionary Society, $3,000 to the Bible Society, and legacies to the cause of education, colonization, Sabbath-schools, seamen, temperance, the widow, the orphan, and other benevolent objects.

It has been well said that he was "every way an eminent man. His character was uncommonly consistent and symmetrical. He moved among his fellow-men as a humble follower of his Saviour, and sunk to rest at the close of his long and useful life, with his hopes stayed alone on the righteousness of the Redeemer." Long a deacon of the Central church, of which the Rev. Dr. Hawes is pastor, he officiated at the communion two weeks before his death.

At a meeting of the bar, after some of the oldest members had borne their testimony to his worth, a younger member stated that he was a teacher in the Sabbath-school for twenty-seven years, and was always at his post prepared and ready to impart instruction, as eminent for his biblical as his legal knowledge.

FROM

REV. DR. DE WITT'S STATEMENT,

AS CHAIRMAN OF THE EXECUTIVE COMMITTEE OF THE AMERICAN TRACT SOCIETY, AT ITS ANNIVERSARY, MAY, 1862.

During the past year death has removed two of the most devoted friends of the Society, who have successfully filled its presidency, who have occupied the highest places in civil life, and have found it their chief honor and greatest privilege to serve the Redeemer in his church, Chief-Justice Williams and Hon. Theodore Frelinghuysen. The chairman has paid a well-deserved and appropriate tribute to the character of our President recently deceased. In the Christian spirit and character, beautifully harmonizing the graces of the Spirit, and displaying always and in every thing the virtues of the life, there was a close affinity between him and Mr. Frelinghuysen. Meekness, kindness, and humility, never shaken and lost, ever invested them; while in all that respected Christian truth and duty, there was an intelligent firmness under the control of love. With Judge Williams my intercourse was but occasional and brief; the impressions left upon me ever reminded me of Mr. Frelinghuysen, with whom it was my privilege to enjoy an extended and intimate friendship which leaves his memory deeply engraved on my heart. Both these venerable men fulfilled the high trusts in civil life to which they were called with distinguished honor; but they felt it their highest privilege and crowning glory to lie low at the foot of the Cross, and to be found in the communion and service of the church. Such was the beautiful simplicity and transparent loveliness and consistency of their Christian spirit and course, that an ordinarily gainsaying world stood admiring and approving. As they were assimilated in life, so were they in their death, occurring within a few months of each other. Their end was perfect peace.

FROM

Hon. ROB'T C. WINTHROP'S ADDRESS

AT BOSTON.

I cannot forget, in entering on the discharge of my duties, (as chairman of the anniversary at Boston,) that the year which has elapsed since your last anniversary meeting has witnessed not a few changes in your official roll. The late venerable President of the association has been called from these earthly scenes within a few months past to enter, as we trust, upon the rich rewards of a long and useful life. His place has already been filled, at the late meeting of the Society at New York, where tributes of the most enviable character have been paid to his memory. But it becomes us here also to give at least some passing expression to our sense of the loss which we have sustained by the death of so distinguished a son of New England.

Few men, of our age and generation certainly, have left a more precious memory in the hearts of good men throughout the country, than the late Chief-Justice Williams of Connecticut. The eminent places which he had held, in so many different spheres of public duty, form but the slightest part of his claim to the remembrance of posterity. I will not attempt to recount them; for official position, alas, has ceased to furnish any safe criterion of private virtue or personal merit. But his pure and spotless character, his noble illustration of Christian principle, his untiring activity in every good work of philanthropy and benevolence, and the signal liberality of his contributions, both living and dying, to so many of our greatest and best institutions for the promotion of moral and religious improvement, will secure an honored place for his name among the benefactors of our land.

PRESIDENT

OF THE

AMERICAN TRACT SOCIETY.

Judge Williams was elected President of this Society, May, 1848. On taking the chair at the twenty-seventh anniversary, May, 1852, he presented the following admirable summary view of the Society's history, principles, and operations.

Under the smiles of a beneficent Providence, we are met once more upon an anniversary of the American Tract Society. Grateful for the success which has crowned the labors of the past, we commence the duties of another year with devout supplications that wisdom may be imparted to those who direct the concerns of the Society, so that all that they do may be done with a simple desire to please God and do good to men.

It will not, I trust, be deemed inappropriate to the occasion to look back to the formation of this Society, and glance at some of *its prominent measures, its progress, and its prospects.*

Little more than a quarter of a century since, a few pious gentlemen of this city observing how the increase of our population exceeded the increase of religious instruction, and how many of our people seldom or never heard the living preacher, met to consult as to the best mode of meeting this state of things.

They could devise no better way than by the distribution of Tracts through our extended country. Something of this kind had been adopted at the time of the Reformation, and infidel philosophers had made use of similar means to effect that great revolution in France which has since had such a prodigious effect upon the world. There were indeed Tract Societies at that time in some of our own states, but having no bond of union, with few exceptions their influence could not be extensive.

It was thought therefore desirable that an institution should be formed in some commercial city, which should unite the whole Christian community who professed evangelical sentiments in one common effort for the diffusion of those great religious truths in which they agreed; and that the commercial metropolis of our country should be the place of its location, that from this great centre of business a circulation might easily be diffused through every part of our country and perhaps the world itself.

After consulting with some of like sentiments from other places, and particularly with those who were connected with other societies then existing, a public meeting was held at the City Hotel in this city, on Wednesday, the 11th of May, 1825, where the American Tract Society was organized, and a constitution formed, under which with some slight alterations the Society now acts—no act of incorporation having been obtained until sixteen years after.

The object of the Society, as expressed in the constitution, was "to diffuse a knowledge of our Lord Jesus Christ as the Redeemer of sinners, and to promote the interests of vital godliness and sound morality by the circulation of religious tracts calculated to receive the approbation of all evangelical Christians;" and to secure this end, the officers and directors were to be chosen from different denominations of Christians, and the Publishing Committee was to contain no two members of the same ecclesiastical connection. And more completely to guard a point so delicate, it was provided that no tract should be published that any one member of this committee objected to. Upon this Publishing Committee and the Corresponding Secretary the labor and responsibility of the publications rest.

At the head of this committee was first placed the venerable Dr. Milnor, whose memory will be ever dear to the friends of the Society for his sound judgment, his comprehensive views, his ardent zeal, and his untiring labors in the Tract cause, to which, as chairman of this committee for twenty years, he contributed his inestimable services.

Last named on that committee at the organization was the Rev. John Summerfield, a youth of high hopes and splendid endowments, whose eloquent effusions will never be forgotten by those who heard him—when on seraph wings he seemed to soar, as if to join those who already surround the throne where he so soon was called.

> "Early, bright, transient, chaste as morning dew,
> He sparkled, was exhaled, and went to heaven."

The other members of that committee, with the Corresponding Secretary, still live revered and honored, to testify for God and this cause. The part they have borne in this great work remains to be told when their work is ended: long may it be before that time shall come.

The object of the Society thus formed, was extensively approved by the friends of evangelical religion; but the doubts felt by good men as to the permanency of such a union, caused fear and trembling to many hearts. Some Christian men ventured to predict that it could not succeed; but as the Committee in one of their reports say, "the object was undertaken not without humble confidence in God that it originated in his Spirit, and that by his almighty power he would carry it forward;" and much prayer went up to heaven for its prosperity.

The danger anticipated was, that there would arise conflicting opinions among the members of the various denominations of which the officers were to be composed, which would interrupt the harmony of their counsels and terminate the union so happily formed. It was indeed an experiment of no ordinary character, and much more doubtful as to the result than that of the Bible Society, as it required much more constant care and watchfulness. Success could not be expected without great candor, ardent piety, and heavenly wisdom in those who were to take the lead. But such was the object to be attained, and such the confidence of the religious community in the character of the persons chosen to accomplish it, that the institution has acquired a strength and importance which its advocates dared not anticipate.

By the liberality of friends, principally in this city, the Society were provided with a convenient house and grounds to commence their operations. Several of the most important local Tract Societies consented to unite with and become branches of this Society; so that during the first year this institution received into their treasury above $10,000, and printed about 8,000,000 pages, of which about 3,600,000 were circulated, by sales to existing societies at reduced prices, or as delivered to subscribers and distributed gratuitously.

Soon, however, a deep interest was excited for the 4,000,000 of inhabitants west of the Alleghanies, where the Society had scarcely commenced its operations. This increased the donations of the next succeeding year. Early calls were also made from missionaries for tract distribution in foreign lands, particularly from Ceylon, Burmah, and the Sandwich Islands, affording new evidence of the value of tracts as auxiliary to the living preacher. Thus was attention turned to the circulation of tracts in foreign languages, as well as in foreign countries.

By the liberality of individual friends, the Society were invited and enabled to stereotype some more extended works, such as Doddrige's Rise and Progress, and Baxter's Saints' Rest. The good effects following these and other similar works, led to what has been called the volume enterprise.

A resolution was early passed for a systematic visitation and distribution of tracts to every family of the entire population, who were willing to receive them. The plan of dividing into small districts, and making distribution monthly by members of churches designated for that purpose, was adopted in many places in our country, and has been continued with more or less fidelity to the present time. It was a plan devised with much wisdom, sanctioned by the best spiritual counsellors, and accompanied with many prayers, and no plan could have been better adapted to the object in view.

An army of voluntary agents was thus raised, going about to spread the truth among persons of all classes and all conditions, accompanied frequently by kind attentions, by pious conversation, and prayer. The seed sown in this way has borne much fruit, and many who were ready to say, No one careth for my soul, have been convinced that there was sympathy for them in the heart of the Christian, and to feel it in their own. How many in this way have found the Saviour, is known only to Him who knoweth all hearts.

Very few of those who have heartily engaged in this work, but can testify to the good effects they themselves have witnessed, and we have reason to believe that a great cloud of witnesses will attest to the same before the universe.

The blessing, however, has not been confined to those who received the tracts. The distributer often was quite as greatly blessed. It gave him a deeper interest in the institution in whose behalf he labored, when he saw its results; it made him feel greater responsibility as a member of the church; it led him to sympathize with the poor and afflicted, as well as with the impenitent; and to be more grateful to God for the superior privileges granted to him.

The catholic principle which distinguished the Society opened the way to a more ready and extensive reception of its tracts and books, than would have otherwise existed; and made them welcome to many by whom they would have been rejected, had they come from any single denomination. And while this mode of distribution was found so highly useful in our cities and villages, something of the kind was still more necessary in the great western country, where, from the sparseness of the population and the inability of the people, the living preacher was seldom seen; especially in the valley of the Mississippi, where, after two years' labor, it was said that not one-fourth of the inhabitants were supplied with tracts, and where the population was rapidly increasing. It was thought necessary, therefore, that more should be done for this purpose.

The subject of tracts for foreign countries continued to be powerfully pressed, and the claims of France, Russia, the Mediterranean, Bombay, Ceylon, Burmah, China, and the Sandwich Islands were earnestly presented; so that as early as 1832 the sum of $10,000 was remitted to aid this great work abroad, it being a larger sum than had been devoted to that purpose during the whole period of the existence of the Society. These remittances, however, instead of weakening the resources of the Society, served greatly to increase the receipts of the institution; so that they were enabled, the succeeding year, to double that amount; and in the year next to that, to add one-third more, making $60,000 in three years; and of the last, $5,000 was sent for China, and $5,000 for Burmah.

The volume enterprise, as it was called, now began to assume a more important place in the operations of the Society.

While a short simple story written with the pen of truth, or a few words of exhortation with the spirit of the gospel, might be best adapted to a considerable class of the community, it was believed that larger standard works of great and good men now no more, would better meet the wants of another portion of our people, as they would not only greatly tend to elevate the standard of piety among those now pious, and lead those who were thoughtless to consideration and repentance, but might in a good measure supersede those light and superficial works under the name of literary, which, when not immoral, often tended to false ideas of life, thus producing dissipation of thought and discontent with the dispensations of Providence.

After much consultation with well-informed clergymen and laymen of various denominations, it was determined to republish works of standard religious authors in a form which would attract the attention of those who would not open a book clothed in the homely garb which alone was known here when Edwards gave to the world his life of Brainerd a century ago.

The blessing attending this effort in the cause of truth, called forth loud commendations from the most judicious. "The success of the volume enterprise," says the late lamented Dr. Archibald Alexander, "gladdens my heart every time I think of it, and I sincerely wish, instead of twenty volumes, you had a hundred in circulation;" and every Report teemed with accounts of its multiplied blessings.

Such was the favor with which these books were received, that it became necessary to find some more effectual mode for their extensive circulation. Letters from distinguished clergymen abroad, and information from officers of the institution and others who had been in foreign lands, showing the result of Colportage, together with its peculiar adaptation to the scattered settlements of our country, all combined to recommend a trial of that system to the directors of this institution.

The experiment was made. A few men of devoted piety and ardent zeal were employed, at a very small compensation, to go to destitute portions of the country to sell these volumes to those who could purchase them, and to distribute to those who could not where they were like to do good, to accompany them by their conversation and prayers, and by their Christian demeanor as well as their books to leave an influence which would be felt wherever they went. The effect of the measure was soon visible. The numbers were increased from time to time. These men, with knowledge derived mainly from the word of God, persevered, often with great labor and sufferings, to perform the service they had undertaken, and left impressions upon the hearts, as well as books in the hands, of many who at first rejected them. The friends of the Society were highly gratified by the reports of the labors of these humble messengers, and have encouraged the work by liberal donations for that express purpose, until the number of persons employed for a longer or shorter time were, for the last year, six hundred and forty-three, visiting more than half a million of families, and supplying them with more than six hundred thousand volumes.

The blessed effects of the labors of these men are to be found in many scattered papers of the annual reports of the Society, and in a condensed form in the last annual report, where a history of ten years of Colportage in America may be found, highly interesting to the mere philanthropist as well as the Christian. Those who have read that report need no further evidence of the value and importance of this system, and those who wish for information will there find it.

Much has been done from time to time through this Society, by the liberality of individuals, in stereotyping volumes of standard works, and in premiums for tracts on various subjects, of which that offered for the best treatise upon systematic beneficence has been productive of most marked beneficial effects. It was the means of calling forth more than one hundred and seventy tracts, many of which were highly deserving, and several of which have been published by the Society, calling the attention of the Christian community to a higher standard and more systematic course of beneficence, and already have been productive of much good.

Much valuable instruction has been given by means of annual and other periodical publications, such as the Christian Almanac, which commenced with a moderate circulation and now requires more than 300,000 copies. The Messenger, though in form a newspaper and published monthly, has reached a circulation of about 200,000; and The Child's Paper, yet in the infancy of its existence, has more than 100,000 subscribers. So pure are the thoughts, so wise the sentiments, and so judicious the counsels emanating from these sources, that we may hope for them a still more extended circulation.

The beneficial effects of the labors of the Society have been felt not only in our land, but extensively in foreign countries. Their tracts have taken as it were the wings of the dove and flown to the ends of the earth. All quarters of the globe have become their beneficiaries. And it may be said, that wherever the foot of civilized man has trod, there has been left the impress of this Society. The English language is but one of more than a hundred languages and dialects in which they have, directly or indirectly, proclaimed the news of salvation to lost man. Verily it may be said, their sound has gone forth to all the world.

The review made at the close of a quarter century will afford a fair test of its progress. In the first year of its existence, the donations were about $7,000, sales about $3,000; total, $10,158 78. In the twenty-fifth, the donations were about $106,000, the sales $202,000; total, $308,266 72. In the first year, 8,053,500 pages were printed; 148,000 pages granted; and there were no foreign grants in cash. In the twenty-fifth year, 307,636,200 pages were printed, 58,138,820 pages granted, and $15,000 were remitted to foreign lands.

That these publications were of the character originally contemplated, is proved by the fact that there has been no division of opinion in the committee, consisting of members of different denominations, as well as by the general voice of the public.

The aim of this brief history of the formation and progress of this Society, is to show that the purpose for which it was formed has been steadily kept in view in what had been contemplated. That object we have seen was, to promote the interests of vital godliness and sound morality by means of tracts, and to diffuse a knowledge of the Saviour. To this great object it is believed all their publications have been adapted, whether the broad-sheet, the American Messenger, The Child's Paper, the Christian Almanac, the little duodecimo, or the larger volume; and this object has been pursued with unremitting industry, and with great economy, the Committee rendering their services gratuitously.

Some may even say that the Society is *doing too much.* Will any true Christian say that too much can be done in such a cause? Is there danger that the great truths of religion will be circulated too far, or reach too many hearts; or that too much light will be shed upon the darkness of the world? Let it be remembered, that though some in many countries have been reached, yet but a small part of the population of the globe have as yet heard of the Saviour. The masses, as yet, are ignorant and unenlightened. And how many are there in Christian lands that know not these truths, and how many among professors that need to have their minds stirred up by way of remembrance.

Will it be said you interfere with *the occupation of those who are publishing religious books?* Such an objection would apply to the whole plan of making religious books cheap, the Bible as well as others. It is setting up the interest of individuals against bringing the gospel to the doors of the poor. But a great object of this association is to bring the gospel to the poor as well as the ignorant. For such Christ came; and it will ever be matter of joy to his followers, to bring these glad tidings to those who have not the means, as well as those who have not the heart to seek them. Besides, the funds which have been placed in the hands of the Society, were given for this very purpose. They are but the trustees of the donors, and woe be to them if they do not faithfully execute that trust. And what good man would refrain from giving to this pious object, even if it should interfere with the business or diminish the profits of a friend? Nor would a benevolent heart ever wish that one mind less should be instructed, or one soul less converted, that his own gains might be increased.

Some have feared that the distribution of tracts and books by agents or colporteurs, might interfere with the rights or duties of *the living preacher*. Such agencies are indeed a substitute, and a most important one, for the living preacher, where such cannot be had. But it is intended for his aid—to draw attention to him, and a desire for him; and there is abundant evidence from the testimonies of missionaries, as well as pastors, that such has been the effect. It has been said by some, that the instruction given by such persons might differ from that of the minister, and in this way produce ill consequences. There can be little danger of this, if these are truly pious persons, and great pains are taken to select none other; and no greater danger is to be feared from this source, than from such advice as is constantly given by pious friends or neighbors to those around them. Such advice or exhortations may not always be as sound or judicious as the pastor himself might give, but who for that reason would object to such communications?

Is it objected, that the Society does not send forth its instructions upon *every subject* connected with vital religion and morality? It must be recollected, that it never proposed to publish all truths, but those truths alone in which evangelical Christians are agreed. Of course by the terms of union nothing of a sectional or party character could be circulated. Will any one of the several denominations engaged in this work acknowledge that his own sect cannot endure these great truths, or that their prosperity would be injured by their extensive diffusion? Such an avowal would excite a suspicion that they were conscious that the essential doctrines of the Bible were not in accordance with their views, or that they were more desirous of giving prominence to their own particular sentiments, than to the great truths of the gospel. The Tract Society do not by their publications preclude the circulation of the writings of the best men of their respective denominations, nor do they interfere with them except as the leading doctrines of the gospel will naturally take the first attention of those who are seeking an interest in the great salvation, rather than those minor speculations which divide the Christian community. The great saving truths of the gospel are those which the Society are principally anxious to teach, with the morality connected with them; and while they do not discard all else as wood, hay, and stubble, they regard it as less essential to salvation, and leave it for others.

Is it said that this Society interferes with *other benevolent institutions?* So far from it, it is the friend of all, and may be said to be auxiliary to all. By its lesser tracts it infuses into the youthful mind a thirst for more extensive information, and leads him to wish to drink deeper from the well of life, and thus sends him to education societies to seek their aid. It is an efficient helper to the Bible Society by its commendation of that fountain from which its own streams are derived, and by scattering abroad its leaves with its own publications. The heart of the home and domestic missionary is cheered in his solitary wanderings by such companions as Baxter and Bunyan and Payson, and he often leaves them to preach to congregations he cannot meet. The foreign missionary has often spoken by such men in languages which he very imperfectly understood, and in places to which he could not gain access. The Seamen's Friend Society, and the Bethel Society, and the Home, have all drawn largely upon the Tract Society, and freely acknowledged its assistance.

Wherever it has scattered its leaves it has been for the healing of the nations, and though much may have been lost on the rock or by the way-side, multitudes of living witnesses will testify that much has been sown on good ground, and is bringing forth fruit sixty and a hundred fold.

During the year that is past the prosperity and usefulness of the Society has been greater than ever. The receipts, the number of colporteurs, the circulation, and grants have been increased. Every day brings fresh tokens of the beneficial results from the labors of the Society, and we have abundant evidence that the hand of God has been over us for good. Thousands in this and other lands are praising him for the blessings conferred by this instrumentality. We have indeed been called to lament, during the year past, the death of two of our venerated Vice-presidents, full of years and of honor, and one of the Publishing Committee, whose age and talents gave hope of much longer usefulness. But we know that He who lent them to us can raise up other Alexanders and Morrows and Masons, or he can work by feebler instruments, if it please him.

Confident we are, that though friends die and enemies arise, our course is onward, and He that is mighty is with us. The work will go on, the gospel will be preached to every creature, the kingdoms of this world will become the kingdoms of Christ. To him every knee shall bow, and every tongue confess him to be Lord, to the glory of God the Father.

HON. THOMAS S. WILLIAMS,

LATE CHIEF-JUSTICE OF CONNECTICUT, DIED AT HARTFORD, ON SUNDAY MORNING, DECEMBER 15TH, 1861, AGED 84.

'T is not for pen and ink,
Or the weak measures of the muse, to give
Fit transcript of his virtues who hath risen
Up from our midst this day.

And yet 't were sad
If such example were allowed to fleet
Without abiding trace for those behind.
To stand on earth's high places in the garb
Of Christian meekness, yet to comprehend
And track the tortuous policies of guile
With upright aim and heart immaculate;
To pass just sentence on the wiles of fraud
And deeds of wickedness, yet freshly keep
The fountain of good-will to all mankind;
To mark for more than fourscore years a line
Of light without a mist, are victories
Not oft achieved by frail humanity,
Yet were they his.

Of charities, that knew
No stint or boundary save the woes of man,
He wished no mention made. But doubt ye not
Their record is above.

Without the tax
That age doth levy on the eye or ear,
Movement of limbs, or social sympathies,

In sweet retirement of domestic joy
His calm, unshadowed pilgrimage was closed
By an unsighing transit.
Our first wintry morn
Lifted its Sabbath face, and saw him sit
All reverent at the table of his Lord,
And heard that kindly modulated voice
Teaching heaven's precepts to a youthful class,
Which erst with statesman's eloquence controlled
A different audience. The next holy day
Wondering, beheld his place at church unfilled,
And found him drooping in his peaceful home,
Guarded by tenderest love.
But on the third,
While the faint dawn was struggling to o'ercome
The lingering splendors of a full-orbed moon,
The curtains of his tent were gently raised,
And he had gone—*gone*, mourned by every heart
Among the people. They had seen in him
The truth personified, and felt the worth
Of such a mentor.
'T were impiety
To let the harp of praise in silence lie,
We who beheld so beautiful a life
Complete its perfect circle. Praise to Him
Who gave him power in Christ's dear name to pass
Unharmed the dangerous citadel of time,
Unsullied o'er its countless snares to rise
From earthly care to rest—from war to peace—
From chance and change, to everlasting bliss.
Give praise to God.

L. H. SIGOURNEY.

www.ingramcontent.com/pod-product-compliance
Lightning Source LLC
LaVergne TN
LVHW021431110826
845150LV00007B/2177

9781425506957